I0605748

ICONIC NATIONAL PARKS

YELLOWSTONE NATIONAL PARK

BY EMMA KAISER

Core Library

An Imprint of Abdo Publishing
abdobooks.com

Cover image: Yellowstone National Park is known for its stunning views.

abdobooks.com

Published by Abdo Publishing, a division of ABDO, PO Box 398166, Minneapolis, Minnesota 55439.

Printed in the United States of America, North Mankato, Minnesota.
052025
092025

Cover Photo: Roman Khomlyak/Shutterstock Images
Interior Photos: Shutterstock Images, 4–5, 30, 42 (bottom), 43 (top); Marion Kaplan/Alamy, 6; Red Line Editorial, 9; Jacob W. Frank/National Park Service, 10–11; North Wind Picture Archives/Alamy, 15; Photo Researchers/Science History Images/Alamy, 16; Danita Delimont/Shutterstock Images, 18–19, 23, 45; A. Falgoust/National Park Service, 21; Stan Tekiela Author/Naturalist/Wildlife Photographer/Moment/Getty Images, 25; Bryan Mullennix World View/Alamy, 26–27; iStockphoto, 29; pabst_ell/E+/Getty Images, 31; Ian Dagnall/Alamy, 34–35; Neal Herbert/National Park Service, 37; Robert Harding Video/Shutterstock Images, 39; Janson George/Shutterstock Images, 42 (top); Daniel Osterkamp/Moment Open/Getty Images, 42 (middle); Galyna Andrushko/Shutterstock Images, 43 (middle); Duncan Selby/Alamy, 43 (bottom)

Editor: Christa Evergreen
Series Designer: Marley Richmond

Library of Congress Control Number: 2024949016

Publisher's Cataloging-in-Publication Data

Names: Kaiser, Emma, author.
Title: Yellowstone National Park / by Emma Kaiser
Description: Minneapolis, Minnesota: Abdo Publishing, 2026 | Series: Iconic national parks | Includes online resources and index.
Identifiers: ISBN 9781098297206 (lib. bdg.) | ISBN 9798384919728 (ebook)
Subjects: LCSH: Yellowstone National Park--Juvenile literature. | Volcanic geology--Juvenile literature. | Natural monuments--Juvenile literature. | Scenic landscapes--Juvenile literature. | National parks and reserves--Juvenile literature.
Classification: DDC 978.7--dc23

CONTENTS

CHAPTER ONE
Old Faithful **4**

CHAPTER TWO
History of Yellowstone National Park **10**

CHAPTER THREE
Plants and Animals **18**

CHAPTER FOUR
Recreation **26**

CHAPTER FIVE
Caring for the Park **34**

Park Landmarks 42

Stop and Think 44

Glossary 46

Online Resources 47

Learn More 47

Index 48

About the Author 48

CHAPTER ONE

OLD FAITHFUL

William and his dad arrived at the Old Faithful Visitor Education Center and walked along the boardwalks in the Upper Geyser Basin. They looked out onto a rocky valley surrounded by pine forests and distant mountains. People from around the world crowded the valley. Outside the visitor center, a sign read, "Old Faithful Geyser Next Eruption Prediction: 12:41 PM." "Hurry up, Dad!" William said. "We don't want to miss the eruption!"

Old Faithful Geyser is one of the most popular attractions in Yellowstone National Park.

Yellowstone's park workers have been teaching visitors about Old Faithful since 1887.

William and his dad found a seat on a bench near the geyser and waited. They had learned from park rangers that Old Faithful is one of 500 geysers in Yellowstone National Park. But it is one of only six geysers with eruptions that can be consistently predicted. The famous geyser is called Old Faithful because it has erupted about 20 times per day, or about every 75 minutes, for more than 30 years. The park rangers can predict the next eruption by using a stopwatch and measuring the height and duration of the previous eruption.

After a few moments, mist began to rise from the geyser. Then a large spray of water rose more than 130 feet (40 m) into the air. William stood on the bench to see above the sea of people. Park rangers made sure that everyone stayed on the boardwalks, warning them that it wasn't safe to get too close. The water shooting up from the geyser was about 204 degrees Fahrenheit (96°C), and the steam was more than 350 degrees Fahrenheit (180°C). For nearly four minutes, William watched in awe as the fountain of spray shot above the

WHAT ARE GEYSERS?

A geyser is a spring of water that reaches very high temperatures. Geysers consist of a long chute that runs at least 5,000 feet (1,500 m) down into Earth's crust. Near the bottom of the chute is hot, liquid rock called magma. Magma heats the water in the chute. When the water begins to boil, it shoots toward the surface, causing an eruption of hot water and steam. Once all the water has been released, the eruption stops, and the process repeats.

PERSPECTIVES

ANOTHER WORLD

Many people describe Yellowstone National Park as unlike anywhere else on Earth. Some say it's like stepping into another world. Some springs in the park are vibrant shades of orange, red, and blue. The Grand Canyon of the Yellowstone River stretches farther than the eye can see. Superheated water rises from the ground as steam. When the first European explorers tried to tell newspapers back home about what they saw in Yellowstone, some papers thought they were making it up and refused to print their stories.

geyser's crust. Then Old Faithful went quiet again, waiting for its next eruption.

THE FIRST NATIONAL PARK

Yellowstone National Park stretches across parts of Wyoming, Montana, and Idaho. It was the first national park established in the United States. It was officially declared a national park on March 1, 1872, when Congress passed the Yellowstone National Park Protection Act.

YELLOWSTONE NATIONAL PARK

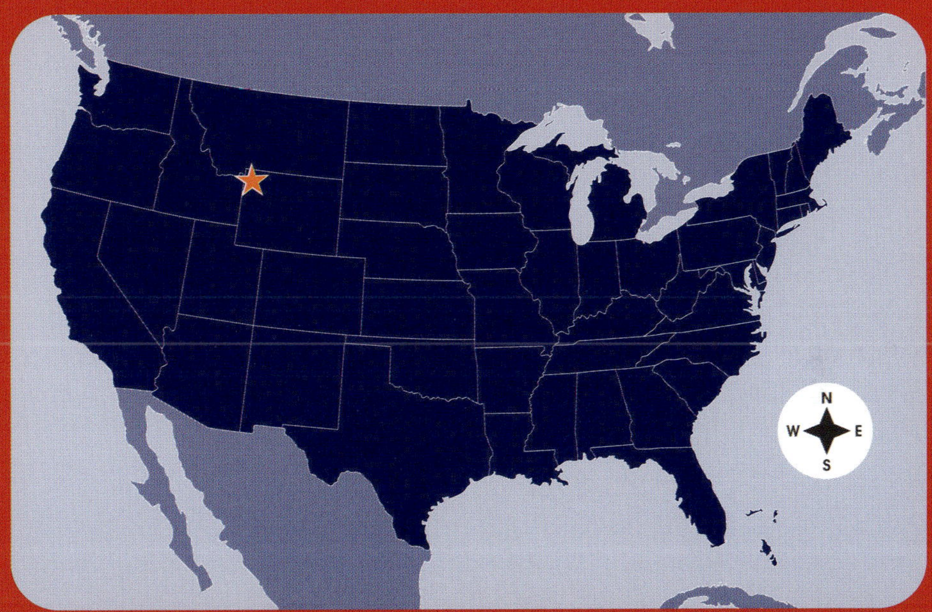

Yellowstone National Park is located in the western United States. Its 2.2 million acres (890,000 ha) span across parts of Wyoming, Montana, and Idaho. What might be some challenges of protecting such a large park?

Yellowstone contains many geothermal and hydrothermal features, along with about half of the world's geysers. About four million people visit the park every year. They come from around the world to see the nature, wildlife, and geothermal wonders in Yellowstone National Park.

CHAPTER TWO

HISTORY OF YELLOWSTONE NATIONAL PARK

People have been living in the Yellowstone region of North America for more than 11,000 years and perhaps as long as 15,000 years. Scientists know this by studying artifacts and the sites where people lived. One of the earliest people groups to live in the area was the Tukudika.

Today, many American Indian nations have connections to the Yellowstone area. Indigenous people have long hunted, fished, and gathered plants in the region.

Today, 27 American Indian nations have connections to Yellowstone National Park.

The Blackfeet, Cheyenne, Crow, Kiowa, Nimiipuu (Nez Perce), and Shoshone-Bannock are among the many American Indian nations that have connections to Yellowstone. The area still holds importance for these nations today.

EXPEDITIONS TO YELLOWSTONE

European Americans began exploring the Yellowstone area in the early 1800s, but the first official expeditions happened around 1870. One of the most important trips was called the Hayden Expedition. It was led by a man named Ferdinand Vandeveer Hayden who worked for the US government. Hayden was accompanied by a team of scientists, artists, and photographers. The team reported back what they saw. A combination of scientific observations, sketches, maps, and photographs helped show people Yellowstone's beauty and importance.

The Hayden Expedition helped convince Congress that Yellowstone should be preserved. Just six months after Hayden returned from his expedition, the US government established Yellowstone as the first national park. This meant that the land within the park's borders could not be owned by individuals.

However, the designation also meant that the American Indian nations who lived on the land were forced to relocate. The US government forced the region's Indigenous people out of Yellowstone and onto far smaller parcels of land called reservations. For the people

PERSPECTIVES

THOMAS MORAN

One of the men who joined the Hayden Expedition was a painter named Thomas Moran. Moran was amazed at what he saw in Yellowstone. He sketched hot springs, waterfalls, and the Grand Canyon of the Yellowstone. When he arrived back home, he finished the sketches and turned them into paintings. These paintings were displayed for Congress. According to Corps of Engineers Captain Hiram M. Chittenden, Moran's paintings "convinced everyone who saw them that the regions where such wonders existed should be preserved to the people forever."

of the American Indian nations who had lived in the Yellowstone region for thousands of years, this meant losing much of their ways of life, including their hunting grounds and places important to their religions.

POACHING

One of the early challenges in managing Yellowstone was preventing poaching. Poaching is the illegal hunting of animals. Bison were a major target for poachers. Some hunted bison for their hides or for sport. Because Indigenous people depended on bison for food, bison were also killed with the intention of weakening American Indian nations. In 1916, only 23 bison remained in Yellowstone. By prosecuting poachers and protecting the remaining bison, park rangers helped bring the species back from the brink of extinction.

MANAGING A NATIONAL PARK

Once Yellowstone became a national park, the US government hired people to take care of the area and make it more accessible to tourists. This meant constructing roads, building park headquarters, and keeping hunters out

Before cars were allowed in the park, tourists came to visit Yellowstone by train, wagon, and horseback.

of the park. Once the railroad arrived in 1883, more people were able to visit. In 1915, the first automobiles were allowed in the park. This gave people easier access to distant parts of Yellowstone.

In 1916, the National Park Service was created to manage US national parks. The organization took over management of Yellowstone from the US Army,

Herbert Hoover visited Yellowstone National Park in 1923.

which had been taking care of the park since 1886. More changes came in 1929 when President Herbert Hoover widened the park's boundaries to include other significant natural areas, such as petrified forests and the headwaters of the Lamar River. Three years later, President Hoover added another 7,000 acres (2,800 ha) to the park. This land provided space for the park's elk to graze.

STRAIGHT TO THE SOURCE

President Ulysses S. Grant officially passed the Yellowstone National Park Protection Act in 1872. The Act declared:

> *The [piece] of land in the Territories of Montana and Wyoming, lying near the headwaters of the Yellowstone River . . . is hereby reserved and withdrawn from settlement, occupancy, or sale under the laws of the United States, and dedicated and set apart as a public park or pleasuring-ground for the benefit and enjoyment of the people. . . . Such regulations shall provide for the preservation . . . of all timber, mineral deposits, natural curiosities, or wonders within said park, and their retention in their natural condition.*

Source: "Yellowstone National Park Protection Act (1872)." *National Park Service*, n.d., nps.gov. Accessed 14 Sept. 2024.

CONSIDER YOUR AUDIENCE

Adapt this passage for a different audience, such as your family or friends. Write a blog post conveying this same information for the new audience. How does your post differ from the original text and why?

CHAPTER THREE

PLANTS AND ANIMALS

Yellowstone is home to a wide variety of plants and animals. The park and the surrounding area, sometimes known as the Greater Yellowstone Ecosystem, are rare because they have not been significantly altered by humans. This has allowed wildlife to flourish. Today, Yellowstone has the largest concentration of wildlife in the lower 48 states.

Plants and animals thrive in Yellowstone in part because of the wide range of habitats

Many tourists come to Yellowstone to see the park's diverse wildlife.

within the park. These habitats include forests, sagebrush steppes, wetlands, and grasslands. These landscapes have formed over thousands of years through volcanic activity, forest fires, earthquakes, and climate change.

PLANTS

More than 1,000 native plant species grow in Yellowstone. Among these plants are hundreds of wildflower varieties. The park is also home to about a dozen types of trees. The most common species of trees in the park are pine, spruce, Douglas fir, juniper, and aspen. These trees make up Yellowstone's dense forests, covering about 80 percent of the park. Shrubs grow in sagebrush-steppe habitats in valleys and along rivers. Wetlands make up only about 10 percent of Yellowstone National Park. However, this habitat is vital for Yellowstone's wildlife, providing homes for 38 percent of the park's plants. About 11 percent of the park's plants can grow only in wetlands.

Yellowstone sand verbena blooms from mid-June until the first frost.

Yellowstone also has three endemic plant species. Endemic species are found only in one place. These species typically live in unique or rare habitats, such as Yellowstone's hydrothermal areas. One such species is Ross's bentgrass. This is a grass that grows in geothermal areas. Yellowstone sand verbena is another endemic species. This plant grows clusters of white flowers and can be found along the shore of

> ## PERSPECTIVES
> ### A DIVERSITY OF WILDLIFE
> **Arthur D. Middleton studies the ecosystems within Yellowstone. He loves studying Yellowstone because of the many species of large mammals. One of Middleton's favorite places to go is the Triad Plateau. This is a very remote area in the southeast corner of the park. He says, "It's truly hard to get to, but up on the Triad you've got summering elk herds, you've got grizzly bears. You can see everything—the Wind River Mountains, the Tetons, the Gravelly Range up in Montana, the Big Horns. It's just an incredible place."**

Yellowstone Lake.

The park's final endemic species is the Yellowstone sulfur wild buckwheat, a yellow flowering plant that grows near the Firehole River.

ANIMALS

About 300 species of birds, 67 species of mammals, 16 species of fish, six species of reptiles, and five species of amphibians live within Yellowstone. The park's hydrothermal features help these species thrive. These features warm the ground in the winter, leading to less

Spring is the best time of year for visitors to see Yellowstone's wildlife.

snow cover. This allows grazing animals, such as bison, to find food. These grazing animals then provide food for larger predators in the park.

Many impressive predators live in Yellowstone. These predators include black bears, grizzly bears, wolverines, wolves, coyotes, mountain lions, and lynx.

Yellowstone is one of the few areas in the United States where both black bears and grizzly bears live together.

THE RETURN OF WOLVES

Wolves once ran wild through Yellowstone, but hunting and habitat loss quickly destroyed their populations. By 1923, no wolves were left in Yellowstone. In 1973, the species became endangered in the United States. Park rangers fought to restore wolves to their habitats. Between 1995 and 1997, 41 wild wolves were brought to Yellowstone from Canada and northwest Montana. The park's wolf population slowly increased. In 2024, there were at least 124 wolves and ten different wolf packs in the park. Scientists study the wolves to learn about their impact on the ecosystem.

It is also one of the only places south of Canada that has a large grizzly bear population. In 2021, there were an estimated 1,060 grizzly bears living in the park.

Seven native ungulate species also live in Yellowstone. Ungulates are plant-eating mammals with hooves. The park's ungulates include elk, white-tailed deer, mule deer, bison, moose, bighorn sheep, and pronghorns.

Yellowstone's wolves control the park's prey populations, keeping the ecosystem healthy.

Mountain goats are non-native but live in northern areas of the park. These species graze on grasses and are common prey for large predators such as grizzly bears.

EXPLORE ONLINE

Chapter Three explores the Greater Yellowstone Ecosystem. The website below goes into more depth on this topic. What information does the website give about Yellowstone as an ecosystem? How is the information from the website the same as the information in Chapter Three? What new information did you learn?

THE GREATER YELLOWSTONE ECOSYSTEM

abdocorelibrary.com/yellowstone-national-park

CHAPTER FOUR

RECREATION

One of the best parts about visiting Yellowstone is seeing the park's unique plants, animals, and landscapes. People come from around the world to explore the park and learn about the region's natural history. Yellowstone has ten visitor centers where people can learn about the park.

Yellowstone National Park also has a rich human history. People can visit the Yellowstone Tribal Heritage Center to learn about the

Yellowstone is one of the most visited national parks in the United States.

27 American Indian nations that are native to the Yellowstone region. Members of these nations come to the heritage center to teach the public about their nations' history, art, and stories. Ranger programs and tours are other great ways to learn more about the park's history.

VIEWING THE SIGHTS

Yellowstone is home to more than 10,000 hydrothermal features, including more than half of the world's geysers. Other hydrothermal features in the park include hot springs, mud pots, and fumaroles, also known as steam vents. These features are all heated by a volcano beneath Yellowstone. Magma heats the water and the ground, creating the hydrothermal features. There are many thermal basins located around Yellowstone. These are areas where several hydrothermal features can be viewed in one place.

One popular basin is the Midway Geyser Basin. There, park visitors can view one of Yellowstone's most

HOW DO HYDROTHERMAL FEATURES WORK?

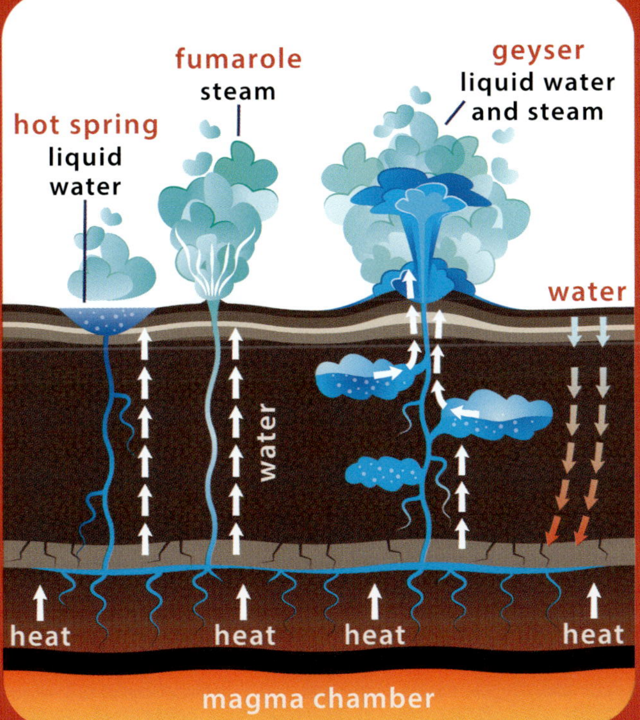

Yellowstone National Park has several different hydrothermal features. How are the hydrothermal features similar? How are they different?

famous hot springs. Grand Prismatic Spring is the largest hot spring in Yellowstone, measuring 370 feet (113 m) in diameter and 121 feet (37 m) in depth. Part of what makes this hot spring so remarkable are the bands of bright orange, yellow, and green that surround

Over thousands of years, hydrothermal features reacted with the rocks that make up the Grand Canyon of the Yellowstone. This turned the rocks orange, brown, and green.

the spring. These bright colors come from bacteria that live in the hot water. Norris Geyser Basin is another popular spot to view hydrothermal features. The basin contains several active geysers.

The Grand Canyon of the Yellowstone is another famous sight in the park. The canyon stretches 20 miles (30 km) long and measures up to 1,200 feet (400 m) deep. It was carved over hundreds of thousands of years by the Yellowstone River.

GETTING ACTIVE

One of the best ways to explore Yellowstone National Park is by hiking the park's winding trails. The park has

Grand Prismatic Spring Overlook Trail leads hikers to a beautiful view of one of the park's most famous hydrothermal features.

more than 900 miles (1,500 km) of hiking trails, with hikes of varying length and difficulty to match each visitor's skill level. Some of the trails are heavily used, while others lead into Yellowstone's less frequented wilderness areas.

Many of the park's trails lead to points of interest. Trails around the Grand Canyon of the Yellowstone provide stunning views of the canyon and waterfalls. Trails around Old Faithful take visitors to hydrothermal features in the Upper Geyser Basin. In the northeast part of the park, trails lead through valleys, mountains, and petrified forests. In the south part of the park, trails take hikers to beautiful lake views.

Many roads and trails in the park are open to bicycles. People can bring or rent bikes to explore the park. Some of the trails are even open to horseback riders. Visitors can take guided tours on horseback or bring their own horses.

Yellowstone is too large to be explored in a single day, so visitors often choose to camp

PERSPECTIVES

STARGAZING

Yellowstone is a great place to view the night sky. The Milky Way galaxy is visible in the park from April to October, and the northern lights can be seen a few times each year. Leslie Quinn works at Yellowstone. She says, "Yellowstone National Park is a good place for stargazing because there are no large population centers nearby. When visitors get a little bit away from the lodges, people are always amazed by the amount of stars they see." Many photographers wait for clear nights to take photos of the stars above Yellowstone's hot springs, mountains, and lakes.

in the park overnight. Yellowstone has 12 campgrounds and more than 2,000 campsites. Almost 300 of these sites are backcountry campsites, which can be reached only on foot or by horse.

YELLOWSTONE IN WINTER

Though many roads close in Yellowstone during the winter, there are still ways for people to explore the park. When snow falls, people can access trails with snowshoes or cross-country skis. Some people even travel to backcountry campsites on skis. With the right gear and preparation, winter visitors can see some truly beautiful views of the park.

FURTHER EVIDENCE

Chapter Four discusses some of the activities available to Yellowstone visitors. What was one of the main points of this chapter? What key evidence supports this point? Read the article at the website below. Does the information on the website support this point? Or does it present new evidence?

THINGS TO DO

abdocorelibrary.com/yellowstone-national-park

CHAPTER FIVE

CARING FOR THE PARK

Though much of Yellowstone's wilderness looks similar to how it did hundreds of years ago, the park has undergone many changes. Several factors impact the park. Climate change, habitat loss, and human activity all affect the Greater Yellowstone Ecosystem.

It can be challenging to keep Yellowstone's ecosystem in balance. This is because all the species in the ecosystem are interconnected. A change in one species can have big impacts

Visitors play an important role in preserving Yellowstone National Park.

on other species. One of the most important parts of managing Yellowstone is making sure the ecosystem stays healthy.

MANAGING INVASIVE SPECIES

Invasive species are species that are not native to an area and cause harm to an ecosystem. Often these species can spread quickly. They outcompete native species, making it hard for an area's native species to survive. This can cause the rest of the ecosystem to suffer. An invasive plant such as knapweed can take over grazing areas, making it hard for native grasses to grow. This then affects the animals that graze on those grasses, such as elk and bison. Without enough food, the grazing species suffer, and their populations decline. This decreases the numbers of available prey for animals such as bears and wolves, causing predator populations to fall.

About 225 non-native species have been found in Yellowstone. Most of the time, people spread

Yellowstone spends up to $3 million each year working to manage lake trout populations.

invasive species. Hiking boots may carry invasive plant seeds, or invasive species arrive in people's cars and boats.

One harmful invasive species in Yellowstone is the lake trout. Since the lake trout was introduced by humans, the fish has outcompeted native species in Yellowstone Lake. The lake trout preys on the native Yellowstone cutthroat trout. This has greatly affected the Yellowstone ecosystem. Many animals, such as eagles, pelicans, otters, and bears, rely on the cutthroat trout as a food source. In 1994, the National Park Service recognized the problem and started a program to control lake trout populations. Since the program's launch, 4.5 million lake trout have been removed from Yellowstone Lake, allowing the native cutthroat trout populations to recover.

A MORE SUSTAINABLE PARK

Over the years, Yellowstone has made changes to reduce waste, use less energy, and be more sustainable. Some of these changes have included increased recycling, upgrading to energy-efficient light bulbs, and installing solar panels. Many of the park's buildings have also been upgraded to require less power for heating and cooling.

BISON MANAGEMENT

Bison are one of the most important species in Yellowstone. The bison in Yellowstone are some of the only descendants of the large wild herds that once roamed North America. In 1902, only 23 bison remained in Yellowstone. Conservation efforts have helped the species recover. Yellowstone now seeks to keep herd numbers between

Visitors should stay at least 75 feet (23 m) away from bison.

3,500 and 6,000. Bison numbers must be managed carefully. If there are too many bison, they will not have enough grazing area within the park. This causes them to travel outside of the park where they are not protected.

One way to manage bison populations is by hunting. Many American Indian nations have long histories and deep spiritual connections with bison.

PERSPECTIVES

YELLOWSTONE'S AMERICAN INDIAN NATIONS

Many American Indians believe they should be allowed to hunt, fish, and gather plants within Yellowstone just as they had done for thousands of years before the park was formed. Others, such as attorney Brett Chapman, believe that the land should be given back to American Indian nations to manage. Chapman said, "The land was stolen and the people who stole it are still in possession of it. I think there needs to be a more frank conversation about what justice mandates."

Since 2007, eight American Indian nations have exercised their treaty rights to hunt bison near the park. The Indigenous people use bison as a food source. They also use other parts of the animal for clothes and cultural traditions. Other American Indian nations play an active role in helping the park manage bison populations and keep the animals healthy.

STRAIGHT TO THE SOURCE

Evan Hubbard started working at Yellowstone National Park in 2016 and eventually became a full-time park ranger. When asked what a day in the life of a park ranger looks like, he said:

> *One of the fun things about being a ranger is that every day is different, especially in the summertime. One day I might be giving an evening talk by the fireside; the next day I'm out managing an animal jam. We have a varying mix of visitors too—from international visitors coming for their first time, to locals who are coming back for the twentieth time. Every interaction is different, and the needs of the visitors are different. That makes every day new—I wake up each morning wondering what the day will bring.*

Source: "NPS Interview: Evan Hubbard, Park Ranger." *Yellowstone Forever*, 25 July 2018, yellowstone.org. Accessed 13 Sept. 2024.

WHAT'S THE BIG IDEA?

Take a close look at this passage. What is the main connection being made between Hubbard's daily schedule and how much he enjoys his job? What do you think makes work as a park ranger meaningful for Hubbard?

PARK LANDMARKS

Old Faithful is one of the most famous geysers in the world. It is known for its consistent, frequent eruptions.

Yellowstone Lake is the largest lake in the park. Even in the summer, the water is too cold for swimming.

Grand Prismatic Spring is the largest hot spring in Yellowstone. It is known for the colorful bands around its diameter.

Mammoth Hot Springs is a large area of hot springs within the park. Rock formations called terraces surround the area's hydrothermal features.

The **Grand Canyon of the Yellowstone** stretches 20 miles (30 km) long. It was cut over hundreds of thousands of years by the Yellowstone River.

The **Yellowstone Tribal Heritage Center** teaches the public about the American Indian nations connected to Yellowstone.

STOP AND THINK

Surprise Me

Chapter Two describes the early history of Yellowstone National Park. After reading this book, what two or three facts about the park's early history surprised you? Write a few sentences about each fact. Why did you find each fact surprising?

Dig Deeper

After reading this book, what questions do you still have about Yellowstone? With an adult's help, find a few reliable sources that can help you answer your questions. Write a paragraph about what you learned.

Say What?

Studying national parks can mean learning a lot of new vocabulary. Find five words in this book you've never heard before. Use a dictionary to find out what they mean. Then write the meanings in your own words, and use each word in a new sentence.

Take a Stand

Many American Indian nations were forcibly removed and lost their land in order for Yellowstone to become a national park. Now some of those nations want to be more involved in the park's management. Some people also think the land should be given back to the park's native nations. Do you think those nations should have a say in how the park is managed today? Why or why not?

GLOSSARY

backcountry
wilderness

conservation
the protection of animals, plants, and natural resources

ecosystem
a community of organisms living together and interacting

expedition
a journey taken for a specific purpose

geothermal
relating to the heat that's produced within the Earth's core

habitat
the natural home of a plant or animal

headwater
the starting point of a river

hydrothermal
relating to water heated by the Earth's core

petrified
describing something that has turned to stone

retention
keeping or holding on to something

steppe
a large, flat, grassy plain

ONLINE RESOURCES

To learn more about Yellowstone National Park, visit our free resource websites below.

Visit **abdocorelibrary.com** or scan this QR code for free Common Core resources for teachers and students, including vetted activities, multimedia, and booklinks, for deeper subject comprehension.

Visit **abdobooklinks.com** or scan this QR code for free additional online weblinks for further learning. These links are routinely monitored and updated to provide the most current information available.

LEARN MORE

Ard, Cath. *Yellowstone*. Flying Eye, 2023.

Hulick, Kathryn. *Camping and Hiking Encyclopedia*. Abdo, 2024.

INDEX

American Indian nations, 11–12, 13–14, 27–28, 39–40
animals, 9, 11, 14, 16, 19, 22–25, 27, 36–40, 41

biking, 32

camping, 32–33
Chapman, Brett, 40
Chittenden, Hiram M., 13

fumaroles, 28, 29

geysers, 5–8, 9, 28, 29, 30, 31
Grand Canyon of the Yellowstone, 8, 13, 30, 31
Grand Prismatic Spring, 29
Grant, Ulysses S., 17

Hayden, Ferdinand Vandeveer, 12–13
hiking, 30–32, 33, 37
Hoover, Herbert, 16
hot springs, 13, 28–30, 32
Hubbard, Evan, 41

Middleton, Arthur D., 22
Moran, Thomas, 13

Old Faithful, 5–8, 31

park rangers, 6–7, 14, 24, 28, 41
plants, 5, 9, 12, 16, 17, 19–22, 24–25, 27, 36, 37, 40

Yellowstone Tribal Heritage Center, 27–28

About the Author

Emma Kaiser is a writer and educator based in western Minnesota. She has a Master of Fine Arts in creative writing from the University of Minnesota, and her writing has appeared in a number of magazines and publications. She is the author of a number of other nonfiction books for students.